DISASTERS

by
Lisa deMauro

to Josh,
whose humor and love
see me through all the tempests

Published by The Trumpet Club
a division of Bantam Doubleday Dell Publishing Group, Inc.
666 Fifth Avenue, New York, New York 10103

ISBN: 0-440-84306-5

Produced by Parachute Press, Inc.
Printed in the United States of America
October 1990

10 9 8 7 6 5 4 3 2 1
CW

PHOTOGRAPH CREDITS

p. 25: top, © 1985 Allan Seiden / The Image Bank; *bottom,* © 1984 David Hiser / The Image
Bank. *p. 26:* © 1983 Don King / The Image Bank. *p. 27: top,* Bob Ellis / Gamma-Liaison
Agency; *bottom,* © 1989 Chuck Kuhn / The Image Bank. *p. 28:* © 1980 Barrie Rokeach /
The Image Bank. *p. 29: top,* © 1989 Kermani / Gamma-Liaison Agency; *bottom,* © Paul
Scott / Sygma. *p. 30: top,* Steve Rockstein / Sygma; *bottom,* © 1989 Tom Knibbs / The
Image Bank. *p. 31: top,* © 1986 Cliff Feulner / The Image Bank; *bottom,* © 1985 Steve
Myers / International Stock Photo. *p. 32:* Randy Taylor / Sygma.

Cover © 1986 Cliff Feulner / The Image Bank

Contents

Introduction   1

Part I The Violent Surface of the Earth   3

  1 Mountains of Fire   7

  2 The Quaking Earth   23

Part II Killer Winds   42

  3 The Biggest Storm on Earth   44

  4 The Whirling Funnel   55

Introduction

The village of Parícutin, west of Mexico City, was a quiet place, except for one thing: Every so often the earth would shake.

And then one day something really unusual happened. On February 20, 1943, a villager named Dionisio Pulido was working on his farm when he heard a noise that sounded like thunder. But it seemed to be coming from *under* the earth. A crack opened suddenly in Pulido's field. Pulido was surprised, but not worried. He kept working until the thunder grew louder and the earth started to shake violently. By that time he *was* frightened.

The land around the crack began to bulge and rise. Soon the mound was taller than Pulido. Next there came a hissing sound as dust, steam, and hot stones began to shoot from the hole and pile up around it. The air smelled like sulphur.

By the next morning there stood a cone 30 feet high—about as tall as a house. A new volcano was born.

Villagers came to watch the eruption, as did scientists and journalists from all over the world. The ground continued to tremble as more ash, rocks, and steam shot from the growing volcano. Some of the rock was so hot that it turned to liquid. At the end of the first week, the cone was 460 feet high and still growing.

The eruption slowed down after the first year. But it didn't come to a complete stop until March 4, 1952, 9 years after it began. By then the volcano had reached a total height of 1,345 feet! (That's just five feet shorter than the World Trade Center towers in New York City!) In that time the small town of Parícutin and the nearby town of San Juan were completely buried.

Since people had plenty of warning, no one was hurt, but many lost their homes and farms. In addition, acres of forest and wildlife were destroyed. Experts say it may take 200 years for the land around the volcano to recover, for new plants to grow, and for animals to return.

Our planet has always been a changing, shifting place. Volcanoes destroy entire towns. Earthquakes cause bridges to collapse. Hurricanes flood thousands of homes and offices and schools. Natural disasters are a part of our daily lives, so we should know what causes them, how they affect us, and what we can do about them.

I

THE VIOLENT SURFACE
OF THE EARTH

If you live on the West Coast of the United States, in Alaska, or Hawaii, your state is home to at least one active volcano. (Alaska has more than twenty-five!) Many of these places are also shaken by frequent earthquakes. But if you live anywhere else in the United States, you're on calmer, steadier ground.

Why do earthquakes happen? To find the answer, take a look at how the earth is put together.

Most of the time, it's easy to think of our planet as a big blue marble. But earth is not a solid ball. It is made up of many layers. The layer where we live—the outer layer—is called the *crust*.

If the earth were the size of an apple, the crust would be about as thick as an apple's skin. In real life earth's crust ranges from a few miles to more than 60 miles thick. Below the crust is a layer called the *mantle*. The mantle contains rock that is so hot, it is melted or *molten*. This molten rock is called *magma*.

Earth's crust may seem like one solid piece, like the skin of an apple before you cut into it. But it's really made up of many different pieces. In that way it's like a soccer ball, which has a solid covering made of pieces of leather that fit together. The pieces of earth's crust are called *plates*. Large and small plates cover the earth.

Earth's plates shift constantly. Most plates move gradually, about 1 to 3 inches a year. When the plates shift suddenly, the earth quakes. And plate movement helps to build volcanoes. The ocean floor shows how.

Sea Floor in Motion

If you emptied the oceans, you'd uncover a world of towering mountains and sharply dipping valleys.

Like the rest of earth's surface, the ocean floor is divided into plates. There is often a ridge line where two plates meet. Molten rock oozes up from beneath the earth's crust. When it breaks the surface of the ocean floor at the ridge, the liquid rock hardens into solid rock.

This new piece of crust pushes the plates of the ocean floor away from the ridge on both sides. The plates start moving in opposite directions away from the ridge, like two huge conveyer belts. Over millions of years, the plates of the ocean floor are pushed toward the continents. This process is called *spreading*.

But the ocean plates can't keep spreading because the oceans are hemmed in by the continents. Often the crust of the continent crumbles into huge chunks that build up and form mountains along the coast.

When a new mountain range is born along the coast, the ocean plate slides under the new mountain range. It slants down into the molten layer beneath the crust of the continental plate. As the ocean plate heads down below the earth's crust, it melts. The trapped magma resulting from the melting ocean crust may then form volcanoes in the mountains along the coast.

This is happening right now along the west coast of North America. The Pacific plate and the Juan de Fuca plate (on which the Pacific Ocean rests) are pushing up against the American plate (on which North America rests), causing mountains to form along the coast. And the Pacific plate has dipped down under the American plate. There it will melt again and add to the pool of magma that feeds the volcanoes along the coast.

Most of the world's active volcanoes appear in a circle surrounding the Pacific Ocean called the "ring of fire." In the next two chapters you'll take a closer look at some volcanoes and earthquakes within the ring of fire. But first you'll relive an eruption that happened long, long ago in the ancient Italian city of Pompeii.

1

Mountains of Fire

If you've got a passport and an airplane ticket, you can travel almost 2,000 years back in time. How? Fly to Italy and head for the ancient city of Pompeii. There you can enter a world where time was frozen in the year A.D. 79 when a volcanic eruption took an entire city by surprise.

The people of Pompeii were living in the shadow of Mount Vesuvius. Everyone knew Vesuvius was a volcano, but no one could remember the last time it erupted. In fact, grapevines and olive trees covered the rich, fertile slopes of the volcano. Flocks of sheep grazed near the mountain's peak. The area seemed perfectly safe. But it wasn't.

On August 24, in the year 79, Vesuvius thundered to life. Around one o'clock in the afternoon a huge explosion was heard throughout Pompeii. Looking toward the mountain, people saw a troubling sign: A large cloud had appeared over the volcano. It was coming from inside the mountain, and it grew larger as the minutes passed.

Was the cloud dangerous? No one seemed to know. A shower of light pebbles began to fall. Some people were frightened enough to drop what they were doing and leave the area right away. But many others stayed, hoping the strange rain of stones would stop and the black cloud would disappear.

Hot ash also began to pour down upon the town. As the ash landed, it set fire to wooden roofs. The day grew dark as chunks of stone began to hail down from the volcano. Now people began to panic. A baker ran from his shop, forgetting the loaves of bread baking in the oven. Roofs began to cave in from the weight of the ash. People had to shake themselves free of the rising ash just to keep from getting stuck in it. The darkness continued because the thick cloud of ash blocked the sun. The air was filled with the sickening smell of sulphur. Poisonous gases pouring from the volcano would prove to be the most deadly part of the eruption.

Many people hid in basements, afraid to go outdoors. In one room sixteen people huddled together along with a dog and a goat, probably hoping to wait in safety until the eruption stopped. But the poisonous gas seeped into the underground room.

Thousands of people raced toward the gates of the city. One woman who tried to escape fell in the street and could go no farther. She covered her head with her clothing to try to keep from breathing the gas, but it was no use. Some people gathered up their valuables. A man who owned a beautiful bronze statue wrapped it in cloth before he fled. But the ceiling of his home gave way, and he was buried with the statue. In another house the owners collected their gold, silver, and jewelry and threw them into a well to keep them safe. But the men ended up falling into the well themselves, overcome by the fumes.

Finally the eruption ended. Buried within a blanket of ash were thousands who hadn't run away in time.

Some citizens who escaped returned after the eruption to dig out their homes. Looters arrived as well, hoping to dig up valuables left behind. But there was poison gas trapped under the ash. Digging in the buried city was too dangerous, so Pompeii was left alone.

As time passed, rainwater soaked into the ash, and a solid covering like plaster formed over Pompeii. The solid ash covering that surrounded everybody and everything held thousands of imprints. An imprint shows the exact shape of the thing it is molded around.

Soon grass grew over the ash. New buildings were erected in the area. People told tales of an underground city, but no one knew exactly where the city was supposed to be.

Then, in the 1590s, some workers who were digging accidentally came upon part of the ruins. Over the years people dug here and there looking for artwork and other souvenirs. During the last 100 years scientists have uncovered Pompeii to see what can be learned from the ancient city.

What they found amazed them. The ash layer had sealed up Pompeii in a natural time capsule. Much of the city was still standing. Homes, shops, and public baths were all there. In some homes tables were set for a meal. There were kitchen utensils, tools, toys, jewelry, and paintings. Advertisements about local elections were written on some of the walls. The loaves of bread left behind by the baker were still in the oven— almost 2,000 years later!

Scientists used the ash molds to make plaster casts of people and even a pet dog who died in the eruption. The plaster casts revealed details about the victims: their expressions, their clothing, and the objects they were carrying. Pompeii was like a treasure chest, filled with lessons about ancient life. The big question is: Could a modern city be caught so completely by surprise?

People know more about predicting eruptions nowadays than the citizens of Pompeii did. In fact, for 17 years *before* Vesuvius erupted, the people of Pompeii and other nearby towns were troubled by many earthquakes. Modern scientists would have understood the connection between these quakes and the volcano. But ancient people didn't know that the quakes were a warning to be taken seriously.

Dramatic volcanic eruptions have led to many legends and beliefs over the years.

• The word *volcano* comes from Vulcan, the Roman god of fire. The ancient Romans thought that Vulcan was a blacksmith who worked inside a mountain making spears, arrows, and thunderbolts for the other gods. Vulcan lived in Vulcano, a volcano on an island near the southern tip of Italy.

• Long ago the Polynesians (and many Hawaiians) thought that Pele, the goddess of fire, caused volcanoes to erupt when she was angry. To keep the goddess happy, people threw pigs or fish into the volcanoes as a sacrifice.

Sleeping Volcanoes

A volcano is considered *active* if it erupts from time to time. A *dormant* volcano is sleeping—it has been active in the past, but is not active now. A volcano that hasn't erupted in recorded history is said to be *extinct*.

Of course, volcanoes don't care about labels. When Vesuvius buried Pompeii, it went from being "dormant" to "active" in one terrifying moment. Even an "extinct" volcano may suddenly spring to life.

But what exactly *is* a volcano? It's a hole or vent in the earth's crust, *and* it's the mountain that forms around the vent. When magma flows up through the vent, it may pour out of the volcano. Lava is simply magma that has flowed out of a volcano.

To understand what makes the magma flow up through the vent in the first place, imagine a pot of soup sitting on a stove. If you heat the pot long enough, the soup will boil. Water in the soup will turn to steam when the temperature rises past the boiling point: 212 degrees Fahrenheit. The steam will rise and the soup will eventually rise up in the pot and boil over.

But what if you put a cover on the pot? The heated steam and boiling soup will have nowhere to go. Pressure will build up inside the pot. If you make a small hole in the middle of the lid, the steam will escape through the hole. Keep adding heat and eventually the soup itself will shoot out, just like a volcanic eruption. (*Warning:* The pot of soup example is too dangerous to try at home as a science experiment!)

Earth's crust is like the tight-fitting lid of a soup pan. When pressure builds up in the superhot molten rock beneath the crust, magma is forced up through cracks or vents in the crust. The result is a volcanic eruption. But what if you have a pot filled with soup, covered so tightly that the soup cannot boil over and no steam can escape? The water in the soup will be hot enough to turn to steam, but there will be no room in the pot for steam to expand. So the water will stay liquid, but it will get hotter than the boiling point of 212 degrees Fahrenheit.

If you take the lid off suddenly, the super-heated water in the soup will turn into steam so quickly that it will explode. This is what happens to the magma that becomes super-heated when it is under earth's crust. Magma is made up of rock and different gases, including steam. Under earth's crust the pressure stops the gases from separating from the rock part of the magma.

But when magma flows through a volcano to the surface, the gases suddenly have room to escape. In very thick lava, the gases actually explode out!

Cones and Mounds

Volcanoes have different shapes as well as different types of lava. The shape of a volcano depends partly on where the vent is located. When most people picture a volcano, they think of a cone-shaped mountain with smooth, sloping sides. This is a *volcanic cone.* One of the most famous is Mount Fuji in Japan.

A volcanic cone is built when lava, ash, and rock flow out of a vent in the center of a mountain. The flow builds up all around the vent in the shape of a cone. Usually, the top of a volcanic cone is a bowl-shaped crater. Volcanoes don't have sharp, pointed tops like some other types of mountains.

Sometimes lava flows out of a long crack along the earth's crust. This is called a *fissure* eruption. Instead of erupting from a hole in the center of a mountain, lava pours out along the crack and covers a large area. It doesn't build a high cone.

Another thing that affects the shape of a volcano is the type of lava, ash, and rock that erupt from it. When lava is thin and flows very fast, it spreads easily. It builds flatter, less steep mountains. Thin lava often forms glowing rivers of liquid rock. You can see this kind of eruption in the Hawaiian Islands, which, like most ocean islands, are built entirely from volcanoes. Lava flows up through openings in the ocean floor. As it cools, it forms a *mound*. Over millions of years the mound grows into a mountain. Eventually it rises above sea level and appears as an island.

Measuring from the floor of the ocean, the highest mountain in the world is a dormant Hawaiian volcano. Mauna Kea (MOW-nah KAY-ah) is 13,796 feet above sea level. But from its base on the bottom of the ocean, it measures 31,784 feet! That's more than 2,000 feet higher than earth's tallest mountain, Mount Everest!

Thanks to its volcanoes, Hawaii is still growing. The state is home to one of the most active volcanoes in the world. Mount Kilauea (kill-ah-WAY-uh) erupted 29 times in a recent period of 25 years. Since the lava is very thin, it flows quickly down the slopes and straight into the sea. There it hardens into new land, extending the island of Hawaii. In a 1960 eruption Kilauea added about half a square mile to the island. Sea water and fiery lava combine and produce miles of black, sandy beaches. One eruption began in 1983, and was still going in 1990. Lava flows destroyed a town that was 20 miles from Kilauea. But the flow was slow enough to give people time to escape.

Thin lava is far more predictable than the thicker, explosive kind. For this reason Hawaiians have been able to live peacefully and even safely with their volcanoes. Tourists and islanders often flock to an eruption to see the light show—from a safe distance.

The thicker the lava, the greater the danger can be. Gases escaping through the thick lava explode from the volcano. When lava is very thick, it doesn't pass easily through the vent. If the vent gets plugged, gases under tremendous pressure build up behind the plug. This can lead to a gigantic explosion. Some explosive eruptions could easily fill 2,000 football stadiums with rock, ash, and dust. A chunk of rock bigger than a bus can be launched as far as 3 miles in a powerful eruption!

Exploding Island

Krakatoa was a small, quiet Indonesian island covered with lush greenery, several square miles in area. No one lived there, but the island was home to a small string of volcanoes.

Krakatoa's volcanoes had been quiet for about 200 years. Then, in the late 1870s, a series of small earthquakes shook the area around Krakatoa. On May 20, 1883, the volcanoes on the island started to shake with explosions.

The eruption seemed like a lot of noise and ash, but nothing terrribly dangerous. Then on August 26, Krakatoa roared to life. Beginning at 1 P.M., thunderous explosions could be heard about every 10 minutes. In a town 90 miles away, the explosions sounded like gunfire. A black cloud rose 15 miles above the island.

As the hours passed, the explosions grew louder and more terrifying. By 3 P.M. the explosions were heard 144 miles away. The air was thick with sulphurous fumes. Dark, threatening clouds loomed overhead. Lightning flashed constantly.

In the middle of the night, there was quiet for a while. But the terrifying explosions began again around 5 A.M. on the morning of the 27th. The loudest of these was heard near Madagascar, more than 2,900 miles from the volcano!

A few hours later it was all over. About two-thirds of the island of Krakatoa had been blown away. The small piece of island remaining was a heap of ash and rock. A tiny nearby island had disappeared completely, and two other small islands grew in size.

Krakatoa was a huge disaster for the people who lived in the area. The power of the eruption set off tremendous waves that washed away whole towns. The final number of deaths totaled over 35,000.

The effects of the Krakatoa eruption reached nearly everyone on earth at that time. Ash from the volcano traveled around the globe and stayed in the sky for years. Sunrises and sunsets glowed with unusual brightness and color. Often the sun appeared to be blue or green. In some places the sky appeared to be gold, deep red, and olive green at the end of the day.

Krakatoa's ashfall also affected temperatures around the world. The blanket of ash blocked about 10 percent of the sun's rays and brought colder weather during 1884 and 1885.

Reading the Signs

Modern science has no power to stop volcanoes and very little power to control their effects. But what about predicting eruptions?

The Cascades are a string of volcanoes beginning in northern California, running north through Oregon and Washington and across the Canadian border. Washington is home to the tallest of the Cascade Mountains, Mount Rainier, which rises 14,410 feet above the ground. Located about 50 miles southwest of Rainier, Mount St. Helens stood almost 10,000 feet high. Covered with forests, meadows, icy streams, and plunging waterfalls, Mount St. Helens was a home to wildlife. Five miles north of the mountain was Spirit Lake, filled with pure, cold water.

Most people around the world had never heard of Mount St. Helens before 1980, when it awoke from a "sleep" of 123 years. But *geologists*—scientists who study the earth—had long been interested in the volcano. And they were using *seismic* instruments to check for volcanic activity. The word *seismic* refers to earthquakes or other movements of the earth's crust. A *seismograph* is an instrument that measures seismic activity.

Geologists kept an eye on Mount St. Helens as it gradually came to life. They planted seismic instruments all over the peak. In the late 1970s geologists warned that the mountain would probably erupt within 100 years and possibly even before the year 2000. Studying past eruptions, scientists also guessed that the lava from the mountain would be the thick, explosive, dangerous kind.

On March 20, 1980, a seismograph showed that a very small earthquake had taken place not far from the mountain. Geologists sprang into action. They began to watch the mountain very carefully. Within days there were more quakes, even closer to Mount St. Helens. To experts, this meant that magma deep underground was moving toward the volcano.

On March 27, 1980, the mountain exploded. Ash and steam rose thousands of feet into the air. And a new crater appeared on the mountaintop. People who lived very close to the volcano were told to leave the area, for safety's sake. Only scientists and law enforcement officers were allowed within 5 miles of the peak.

One of the chief watchers was a thirty-year-old government geologist named David Johnston. Johnston loved volcanoes so much that he was willing to risk his life to study them. He lived in a camp in the shadow of Mount St. Helens, watching the mountain, and waiting for something to happen.

One day the mountain began to bulge on its north side. Magma and gases were building up under pressure. The bulge expanded like a balloon. Sooner or later the bulge would have to burst. Johnston and fellow scientists moved their camp 5 miles away, to a place that was supposed to be safe.

On May 7 the volcano erupted again, but the bulge stayed where it was. One scientist predicted that the big eruption would come on May 21.

On May 18 David Johnston was up early. He was all alone at the geologists' camp. Then suddenly earthquakes shook the ground and the bulge gave way. Johnston grabbed his two-way radio and shouted with excitement to his fellow scientists in Vancouver, Washington, "Vancouver! Vancouver! This is it!" And with that, David Johnston disappeared. In the first moments of the explosion he and his camp were obliterated from the face of the earth by the impact of the eruption. His body was never found.

Tons of rock slid down the side of the mountain. The trapped magma and gases exploded outward traveling at 200 miles per hour. The wind carried chunks of rock, some as big as cars. A combination of wind and rock flattened trees and anything else in the way for 20 miles.

Three days after the blast, ash was raining down on the eastern states. Two weeks later it had traveled around the world. The mountain had hurled out more than a ton of ash, rock, and mud for every single person on earth!

For all the warnings, more than sixty people were dead or missing. Some people had ignored roadblocks because they thought that taking a risk was exciting. Others were trapped while camping or hiking.

Most of those who lived near the mountain lost everything *but* their lives: their clothing, cars, furniture, toys, and not just their houses but the land itself. The grass and trees turned into a gray, mud-covered wasteland. Damages to crops, property, and industry were thought to be more than $2 billion.

What remained of a beautiful mountain was ash-covered rubble. The water was boiling mud. The wildlife was dead. The forests were gone. Spirit Lake looked like a scene from a battlefield, surrounded by steaming vents.

Mount St. Helens showed us just how far we are from understanding volcanoes. The mountain was easy to watch. Many of the best geologists in the world were studying it. And yet, no one really knew what the mountain would do.

Life Returns

It's easy to view a volcanic eruption as a destructive event. And, of course, in many ways it is. And yet, volcanoes do not just destroy, they build and rebuild.

Volcanoes create new land as often as they destroy old land. Take away the volcanoes and there wouldn't be tropical islands. Although the beautiful Cascade Range could be destroyed by volcanic activity, it would never have existed at all without eruptions.

The lava and other material that erupts from a volcano also make for very fertile soil. That's the reason that the Pompeiians were farming and living so close to the crater of Vesuvius. And that's why Mount St. Helens was such a lush, green wilderness.

People have learned to put volcanoes to work. Iceland is built mostly of volcanoes, and it experiences many eruptions. But the people of that nation put the earth's energy to good use. They use underground water that is heated by super-hot magma. Pipes that carry the hot water into homes supply inexpensive, pollution-free heat for the Icelanders.

Today millions of people live near active volcanoes. Though eruptions are much more predictable than they used to be, volcanoes are still a daily threat. Even if we can't control them, we can learn to appreciate and even use the powerful forces that form our planet.

2

The Quaking Earth

San Francisco is located on the Pacific Coast of the United States. The land around the Pacific Ocean is part of the ring of fire, known for its active volcanoes and earthquakes. San Francisco is not in the shadow of any active volcanoes—the nearest one, Lassen Peak, is about 250 miles away. But San Francisco has had more than its share of earthquakes.

City on the Fault Line

The city is built where the North American plate meets the Pacific plate. This area is criss-crossed with cracks in the earth's crust called *faults.* The pieces of land on either side of a fault move in different directions, at different speeds. The biggest of the faults in the network is the well-known San Andreas Fault.

The San Andreas Fault runs on or near much of the coast of California. It begins inland from Los Angeles, which is west of the fault. Then it heads north toward San Francisco, which is just east of the fault line. Just below San Francisco it runs into the ocean and continues offshore.

What happens along a fault line depends on which way the pieces of land are moving. When a plate under the ocean pushes against a continent, the ocean plate slides under the continental plate. Mountains can form along the coastline from the rising land.

Two plates can push right into each other, like two cars in a collision. Over millions of years continuous head-on movement often pushes up mountain ranges. The Himalayan (hih-MAHL-yin) Mountains of Asia were formed that way. One plate (where India is today) pushed into another plate (where China is today). The crust rippled and rose into towering mountains at the point where the two plates meet. Mount Everest, the tallest peak in the world, is part of the Himalayan range.

Of course, Mount Everest wasn't built in a day! The two plates probably first met more than 40 million years ago at sea level. As the plates came together, part of the ocean floor was included in the rising mountains. Scientists have found fossils of animals that once lived underwater preserved in the rocks of the highest mountain range on earth!

Mount Fuji, a stunning volcanic cone topped by a bowl-shaped crater, towers over Yamanaka Village in Japan.

Thousands of years after Mount Vesuvius erupted, scientists were able to make plaster casts like these from the imprints of bodies left in the ash of Pompeii.

Fiery lava shooting from Mount Kilauea in Hawaii in April 1983.

In 1980, Mount St. Helens awoke from a "sleep" of 123 years. Smoke billowed from the newly active volcano.

Nearly 2,000 feet of mountainside were blown away from the north face of Mount St. Helens during the eruption!

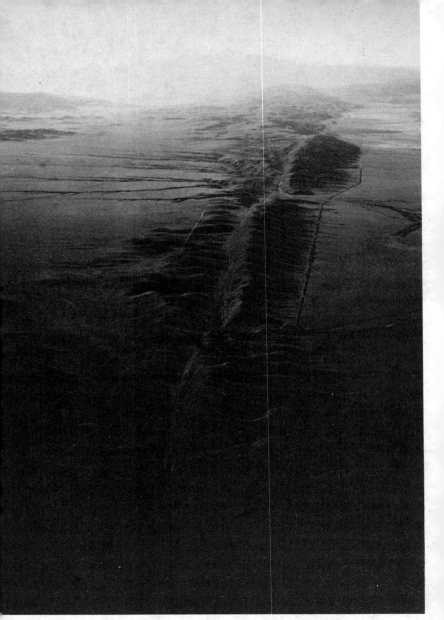

This is an aerial view of the San Andreas Fault in California. Plate movement along the fault beneath Earth's surface causes earthquakes.

The tremors that shook San Francisco in October 1989 caused this giant crack to appear in the pavement.

Victims were trapped in cars when the top level of the Nimitz Freeway collapsed during the 1989 San Francisco quake.

The fierce winds of Hurricane Hugo hit the island of St. Croix in September 1989.

In Charleston, South Carolina, Hugo's high tides carried this sailboat inland and stranded it in the middle of a road!

Take cover in the cellar—a tornado is approaching this Illinois farmhouse!

This big motor home was picked up in the air and plunked down on a tree by a tornado!

Tornadoes can cause wood to punch holes in steel.

Sometimes two plates move horizontally against each other, the way your hands move back and forth when you rub them together to warm them. This is happening along the San Andreas Fault. If two pieces of land move side by side, they don't push up mountains. The movement is so slow that no one who lives on the moving land really notices it. Los Angeles is moving toward San Francisco at the rate of about 2 inches a year!

The effects of plate movement aren't always dangerous. A road running across a fault line may get cracks in it from being slowly pulled in two directions at once. A row of trees may not quite line up after many years of plate movement. The big danger doesn't come from the slow, gradual movement of plates. Problems occur when plates *cannot* move smoothly side by side.

As a plate moves an average of 3-thousandths of an inch a day, the layers of rock in the crust rub against each other. They catch hold of each other and lock part of the plate in place. But the plate is still being pushed, even though it can't keep moving. Every now and then the pressure becomes too great. The plate shudders or jumps forward into a new position, resulting in an earthquake.

Earthquakes can and do strike almost anywhere on the surface of the planet. And they strike without warning, which adds to the danger. Over the centuries, these "sneak attacks" have led to some strange ideas about earthquakes.

• People once thought the earth rode on the back of a giant tortoise or frog. When the animal moved, so did the earth.

• People believed that earthquakes were a punishment for bad behavior.

• Animals are thought to know when an earthquake will happen. Dogs bark wildly or act scared; birds flutter strangely. In one ongoing study, cockroaches *do* seem to move around much more right before a quake.

Measuring Quakes

The measurement scientists use for earthquakes is called the *Richter scale*. Each number on the scale from 0 to 9 stands for a quake that is 10 times bigger than the number before it. For example, a quake that measures 6 points on the Richter scale is 10 times bigger than a quake that measures 5. A 7 is 100 times bigger than a 5.

Not every earthquake is a terrifying event. Scientists guess that people feel hundreds of thousands of tiny earthquakes every year. Many more are so small that no one can feel them.

The First Big San Francisco Quake

A police sergeant was patrolling the empty streets of San Francisco at five o'clock in the morning on April 18, 1906. Suddenly the impossible was happening: The earth beneath his feet began to move. The pavement rippled like water on a stormy sea.

The air was filled with a powerful roar. Everything solid was suddenly moving: Buildings swayed. Sidewalks buckled. Windows shattered. Bricks rained down.

The big earthquake was over within minutes. But the danger—and the destruction—had just begun. Chimneys, walls, sidewalks, and bridges were not the only thing to be torn apart by the quake. The pipes that carried fuel gas into San Francisco homes were split open. Gas leaked out and burst into flames almost immediately.

Water pipes were also shattered. Water gushed uselessly into the broken streets. As blazes were breaking out all over the city, there was no water left in the pipes to put them out. Fire fighters pumped water out of the sewers. Wherever possible, they pumped water from San Francisco Bay. And yet block after block was swallowed up by the flames.

People sat in their homes waiting helplessly. They knew that within minutes the flames would arrive. Some tried to load their valuables onto wagons, but horses were scarce. Besides, there was nowhere to run. No part of the city was safe from the raging fires.

For 3 days and nights, the city was a smoky nightmare filled with flames. When the last of the fires went out, officials counted the victims. As many as 3,000 people may have lost their lives in the quake and the fires that followed. Almost 250,000 people lost their homes in addition to their jobs, shops, schools, and libraries.

The people of San Francisco began to rebuild their city almost immediately. Within a few years the burned-out city was filled with new homes, offices, and stores. But the lesson of 1906 was never forgotten.

Scientists estimate that the San Francisco earthquake measured about an 8.3 on the Richter scale. And since the conditions that led to that quake haven't changed, the people of San Francisco have always lived with the idea that another big one could hit at any time.

But earthquake science has come a long way since 1906. Experts have learned how to build buildings that will be less likely to collapse. They have invented better systems of carrying water and gas, so that fire will not do so much damage. Scientists saw their safety measures put to the test when a major quake jolted the city on October 17, 1989.

San Francisco, Again!

During World Series week in October 1989, baseball fans in California were very excited. The championship was being played out between the San Francisco Giants and the Oakland Athletics, two teams from the same metropolitan area.

It was early evening. Candlestick Park in San Francisco was full. About 58,000 fans were waiting for the third game in the series to begin. Many more fans in the area left work early to get home to watch the game on television.

Sixteen minutes before the game was due to start, the earth rumbled to life. Towers in the stadium began to sway. Chunks of concrete broke off the sides of the stadium and fell to the ground. People screamed. San Francisco was having an earthquake and it was a big one: 7.1 on the Richter scale.

News of the earthquake spread instantly across the nation. Many Americans were tuned in to televisions or radios for the baseball game. When the quake came, they learned of it right away. But it took several days before anyone could figure out exactly how many people had been hurt or killed.

Many victims of the quake were trapped in cars between two levels of an interstate highway. Pieces of the highway's top level fell right onto the bottom level, crushing the cars that were caught in the middle. No one knew how many were trapped up there until the rescue work was completed.

Olidean Harvey was one of the luckier highway commuters; she was on the upper roadway during the quake. When the earthquake first hit, she thought she had gotten a flat tire. "Then I looked in my rearview mirror and saw the freeway coming at me like a wave. The freeway started to go up and down, like waves on the ocean," she said.

Many riders trapped between the two levels of the highway were badly hurt. It was difficult and dangerous for rescue workers to try and reach them. People had to climb up to the damaged roadway, using ladders or cranes. Often they had to crawl into spaces only 2 or 3 feet high, not knowing if an aftershock—a smaller quake—might cause the whole highway to crumble. Also, the smoke from cars that had caught fire filled the air and made many of the victims and rescuers very sick.

And yet people *did* risk their lives to help: Doctors treated victims who were still trapped in their cars. Others used machinery to cut away parts of the crushed cars to get the trapped people out.

Early reports said that as many as 300 people might be dead. Fortunately, the final count was less than 70. Experts say the number was lower than expected because so many people in the San Francisco area had gone home early to watch the ball game. The World Series actually saved many lives!

Walls of Water

California is not the only state that suffers earthquakes. On March 27, 1964, an earthquake shook Anchorage, Alaska. It rippled through the streets, killing nine people. Three-quarters of the city's property was destroyed. But the real threat of the quake came after the shaking stopped.

Large pieces of the ocean floor around Alaska had been moved by the quake. All of the underwater movement caused huge waves called *tsunami* (soo-NAH-mee) to form. *Tsunami* are not the same as tidal waves. Tidal waves are produced by tides. *Tsunami* result from the impact of earthquakes and volcanoes on the ocean.

The giant waves began to appear, about one an hour. They bombarded the Alaskan coast. Some of the waves were 30 feet above the high-water mark! They washed over harbors and towns and carried away houses and piers. In Seward storage tanks holding 40,000 barrels of oil collapsed. Oil poured into the water and caught fire. When the giant waves hit Seward, they washed blazing water over the town. In all, 118 people died in the quake. It was the largest quake ever measured in the United States: 8.5 on the Richter scale!

Quakes Everywhere

It isn't just the ring of fire that feels the effects of earthquakes. There are hidden fault lines all over the earth, not just on the edges of plates. In the United States earthquakes are sometimes felt in Massachusetts and New Jersey. And one of the biggest earthquakes in American history took place in the town of New Madrid, Missouri.

On December 16, 1811, the air was suddenly filled with thunderous noise for miles around New Madrid. Trees split and the Mississippi River seemed to boil. The rumbling and shaking continued on and off for more than four months! The movement could be felt in New York City and in Charleston, South Carolina.

When the quaking stopped, New Madrid was destroyed. The effects of the quake were felt in other states as well. An 18-mile-long lake had been created in Tennessee where the land sank and filled with water!

The Next Big One

Most experts feel it will be a long time before anyone can predict an earthquake accurately. In the meantime, scientists can often guess which areas are *likely* to have a major earthquake by studying past quakes and by taking note of areas that seem overdue for a quake. These predictions are helpful in planning for an earthquake.

By carefully noticing the type of earthquakes that happen at different points along a fault line, experts can recommend the safest places to build new schools, nuclear plants, dams, and tall buildings.

Scientists can also use instruments to watch a small area very closely. They take constant readings of movements of the earth's crust. This may make it possible for them to give a warning of 30 to 90 seconds before an earthquake hits. Unfortunately, this is not enough time to be useful to most people.

For years many scientists said that California would probably be hit by a major quake sometime before the end of the twentieth century. The Los Angeles area, home to about 13 million people, is one spot that might suffer an earthquake disaster. And, of course, San Francisco is another likely target. The 1989 earthquake relieved some of the pressure that was building up along the fault line. Was that the last quake for a while? No one can say for sure.

II

KILLER WINDS

Imagine a hot, sunny summer day. You swim in the blue ocean beneath thick, billowy white clouds. You head back to your blanket and lie down. After a few minutes you doze off.

Crack! A huge clap of thunder shakes you awake. The sky is steel gray. In the distance a white-hot flash of lightning rips through the sky.

What happened? The answer will sound like a weather forecast you hear on the news: A low-pressure parcel of moist, warm air rose into a high-pressure layer of cool, dry air.

Highs and Lows

When sunshine warms a section of air, the molecules in the air move more quickly and spread out. They are not so densely packed together, and there is more room between the molecules. So a parcel of warm air tends to be a low-pressure area, or "a low." In cold air, molecules move around less. They stay more tightly packed, and they exert pressure on each other, like people stuffed into a crowded elevator. So a parcel of cold air is a high-pressure area, or "a high."

What if a crowded elevator stops and the doors open suddenly onto an empty hallway? The people in the elevator spill out into the hallway. The same thing happens when a high comes up against a low: The high flows toward the low.

Since there are fewer molecules in a low than in a high, a low is lighter than a high. And that's why warm air tends to rise. When warm air rises, cooler, heavier air will usually move in to take its place. When cool air moves in to fill a space that has been left open by rising warm air, we feel a breeze. If the air rises quickly, we feel a powerful wind.

There are only a few basic ingredients that make up all the different types of weather we experience: temperature differences, moisture in the air, and high- and low-pressure areas. When these ordinary weather conditions come together in a very special way, the results can be dramatic hurricanes and tornadoes.

3

The Biggest Storm on Earth

Christopher Columbus hoped to find a new route to Asia when he sailed west from Spain in the 1490s and early 1500s.

What he found instead surprised him: lands no one in Europe had ever heard of; seas no one had ever charted; and *terrifying* storms. These huge windstorms were more powerful than anything Europeans had ever seen. The native people he met told him that these storms were sent by a mighty storm god: Hurakán.

Five hundred years later we still call this kind of storm a *hurricane*. (If it appears in the Eastern Hemisphere, then it's called a *typhoon*.) And we are still amazed at its size and power. We now know that in one day a hurricane may release more energy than the total amount of electrical power the United States uses in a year. And it may cause a rainstorm equivalent to 10,000 gallons of water for each person on earth.

In September 1989 weather scientists were keeping a careful watch on a storm that was becoming bigger and stronger as it moved across the Caribbean Sea. By the middle of the month Hurricane Hugo was headed straight for Guadeloupe, the Virgin Islands, and Puerto Rico.

Scientists knew that Hugo was dangerous. It had winds of more than 130 miles per hour. People were told to leave their homes near the coast and get to higher ground.

When the hurricane hit, it was fierce. Trees snapped and were sent whipping through the air. Windows shattered. Thousands of houses were destroyed. After Hugo left the islands, it moved toward the U.S. mainland.

On September 20, experts were warning people that Hugo would probably hit the East Coast of the United States somewhere between northern Florida and North Carolina. But there was always the chance that the storm would blow harmlessly out to sea.

Around midnight on September 21, Hugo slammed into Charleston, South Carolina. The winds measured 135 miles per hour! They toppled trees and power lines and left bridges twisted and broken. Rain and the seawater driven by the storm flooded huge areas and wrecked buildings. Boats were lifted by the high tides and carried inland, where they were stranded on lawns or streets.

Hugo did tremendous damage in both North Carolina and South Carolina. Luckily, most people listened when the experts said to leave the areas where the hurricane would hit hardest. Seventy-one people died as a result of the storm. Many were killed not by wind or water, but by damaged electrical lines.

One man who did stay in his home through the storm was terrified when his brick fireplace exploded in the wind. He thought the kitchen door might give way, so he pushed his refrigerator against it and waited until the winds died down.

Six billion dollars' worth of property was destroyed in South Carolina alone! Millions of acres of timberland were wiped out. Forest fires became a big threat because of all the fallen trees. Many of the animals that survived the storm starved to death later on.

Help From All Over

Hugo's victims had to face the difficult job of trying to rebuild their lives. The first task was finding food and shelter for the days following the storm. After that would come the bigger task of trying to rebuild homes, businesses, and schools.

People from around the country and around

the world offered to help out. Builders donated materials for rebuilding. A New Jersey town sent 37 truckloads of food and clothes, 3 fire trucks, a dump truck, plus electricians and other workers to help one storm-damaged town in South Carolina.

People attending college football games throughout the southeastern states were asked to bring donations of food, clothing, and money for victims of the storm.

In the Northeast more than $7 million in cash and supplies were donated by caring people for the hurricane victims of Puerto Rico and the Virgin Islands. Teams of New York City fire fighters, police officers, and parks department workers went to help out in Puerto Rico.

Double-edged Danger

Perhaps the most unusual thing about a hurricane is its unique trait of striking twice. For people in the past who couldn't get an overall look at the storm as we can today, the double-edged attack must have seemed very confusing.

First the hurricane would roar over an island with fierce winds and driving rain. Then all would be quiet for minutes or at most a few hours. Then the storm would return, but this time, the winds would blow from the opposite direction. The result: Buildings and trees toppled from the two-way attack.

For those who weren't used to hurricanes, the storm's second attack could prove deadly. People would wait out the first part of the storm in a safe place. Then they would come out into the open during the calm, thinking that the worst had passed. Then the storm would strike again and surprise the unsuspecting victims.

Why does this type of storm have two stages? The winds of the hurricane travel in a circle around the calm center—or the *eye*—of the storm. But the entire storm is constantly moving, across the ocean and on toward land. During a hurricane, first you feel overpowering winds and torrents of rain passing over you from one direction. Then you're in the eye of the storm and the air is calm. Finally the back part of the spiral hits and the winds and rain blow from the opposite side.

Clear Skies, Calm Seas

Another strange fact about hurricanes is that they form only when the weather is warm and calm. The ingredients for making a hurricane are a hot, sunny, windless day and a patch of warm, calm sea.

As the sun shines on the ocean, water begins to evaporate. Gallons of water turn to vapor. Because the air over the water is warm, it rises and carries the water vapor up with it. As the heated air rises, cooler, heavier air moves into the space over the water. Then this process repeats itself.

Because of the rotation of the earth, the air moves in a circular route as it flows into place above the sea. Near the ocean's surface, the air is traveling down and around in a counterclockwise spiral. The air moves in a counterclockwise direction only in the Northern Hemisphere, above the equator. Below the equator, hurricane winds move in a clockwise direction.

As the cool air circles down and around, it squeezes the center where the warm air is rising. The center becomes smaller, and that forces the air to move more quickly. As the air rises more quickly, it pulls in cool air more quickly. This again squeezes the center, so the swirling winds tighten and increase in speed.

The water vapor that is rising in the center will eventually meet cooler air higher up in the sky. Some of the vapor will condense and become liquid again. Clouds will form and move toward the edges. The swirling winds will hold the water-filled clouds. In the storm's center will be the calm, cloudless eye.

When the clouds meet the cooler air around the hurricane, some of the water vapor will begin to fall as rain. An average hurricane may drop about 200 billion tons of water a day as rainfall. After 4 days of rain at that rate, you'd be able to fill Lake Erie.

There are three levels of storms with swirling winds that form over tropical waters. As a group they're known as *tropical cyclones*. The smallest, mildest storm is the tropical depression (winds less than 39 miles an hour). Next comes the tropical storm (winds of 39 to 73 miles an hour). When the winds reach 74 miles an hour or more, the storm is called a hurricane.

But hurricanes can blow a lot harder than 74 miles an hour, which is as fast as a speeding car on a highway. Sometimes their winds are twice that fast or more. In fact, since a hurricane draws its power from the ocean, it tends to grow larger in a larger ocean. As a result, tropical cyclones are bigger when they begin over the Pacific Ocean, where there is more room to grow than on the Atlantic. Winds of 250 miles an hour are not unusual for a Pacific typhoon.

Hurricanes generally lose power over land, especially if they pass over mountains and valleys. If, however, the storm heads back to sea before it dies down, it may "refuel" while over the water, building power by picking up more moisture.

By far the most dangerous result of a hurricane is the flooding. The center of the storm is an area of very low pressure. The heated air in the center expands and rises. It is light and constantly moves up the "chimney" at the center of the storm. Ocean water under the eye of the storm rises a foot or more into the eye. This dome of water may be many miles across. As the hurricane moves toward shallow water, the rising ocean floor forces the dome of water even higher. Ferocious winds whip the water into tremendous waves.

When the hurricane strikes land, this raised section of the sea—known as a *storm surge*—travels inland, bringing flood waters. Ninety percent of hurricane deaths are a result of storm surges. Without warning, the sea covers the land. Homes, trees, bridges, and people are swept away by the water.

A City Destroyed

Galveston, Texas, a city on an island in the Gulf of Mexico, was home to almost 40,000 people in the year 1900. Each summer the population swelled when tourists came. The bustling, wealthy city was the most important seaport in Texas.

Over the years Galveston had withstood many fierce storms which battered the beaches and flooded the streets. But nothing could compare with a storm that headed toward the city on September 7, 1900.

Feathery clouds from the top of the hurricane appeared in the sky. These were replaced by a dark cloud layer. Waves pounded the shore. By the next morning the streets near the beach were beginning to flood. Waves that were being pushed ahead of the storm were reaching 4 feet above the usual high-tide mark. On the morning of the 8th, a driving rain began to pound the city.

As the storm came closer, the tide rose a foot every hour. Driven by fierce winds, the water poured into the city. Soon it would cover the island completely.

Flooded houses collapsed and swirled in the rising water as the rain continued to thunder down. Broken windows and chunks of wood hurtled through the air. A steamship broke loose and crashed through all three bridges that led to the mainland. Winds averaged 84 miles per hour during the afternoon, but gusts came through at 100 miles per hour and more.

Then at 7:30 P.M. the water rose 4 feet in 4 seconds. Terrified people ran to the top floors of their homes, only to have the floors collapse and the pieces float away. By ten o'clock in the evening, the city of Galveston was destroyed. And thousands were dead—probably as many as 7,200.

The survivors rebuilt the city and put up a seawall 18 feet high, taller than the high-water mark of the hurricane's floods. Hurricanes still threaten Galveston, but the wall still stands—and so does the city.

Naming the Storms

During World War II, the idea of using girls' names to label the storms was born. In 1953 the government weather service made it official policy. For years, they chose from several lists of names, beginning each year with the letter A for the first storm and continuing through the alphabet until the last storm of the year was named. The following year they would begin with letter A of the next list of names.

In 1979 the government decided to include boys' names as well. Now each year's hurricanes alternate between male and female names, in alphabetical order.

Learning To Live With Hurricanes

As Hurricane Hugo proved, weather experts have gotten much better at understanding hurricanes, but they can never say for certain what these storms will do. Thanks to the warnings issued by scientists, however, the number of deaths can often be greatly reduced.

Many drownings due to storm surges can be prevented when people in low-lying areas are given time to seek higher ground. In some cases, though, lives that can be saved are lost when people don't listen to hurricane warnings.

In August 1969 Hurricane Camille plowed into the Gulf Coast of the United States. 200,000 people followed advice to cover their windows with pieces of wood, remove or tie down anything that might blow away, and head inland, away from the coastal areas of Mississippi and

Louisiana. But in the small town of Pass Christian, Mississippi, about half the population ignored the warnings.

One group of twelve people decided to hold a "hurricane party." When police told them of the coming danger, they just laughed. All twelve people were killed.

Hurricane Camille was responsible for more than 250 deaths. Many of these people died as a result of flooding and mudslides that followed an unexpected downpour *after* the hurricane had died down. But there's no question that many could have been saved if they had taken seriously the danger of earth's most ferocious storm.

4

The Whirling Funnel

Does the word *tornado* remind you of anything? For many people, it brings to mind one particular tornado: the one from the movie *The Wizard of Oz* that lifted a Kansas farmhouse, sent it spinning high into the air, and set it down in Munchkinland. Of course, in real life, no one ever rode a twister to Munchkinland. But tornadoes *have* caused some pretty strange things to happen.

• A piece of wood, driven by powerful winds, punched a hole in a steel pipe and stuck there. Delicate bits of straw were driven deep into a tree trunk as if they were hard as nails.

• A man, lying asleep in his bed, was lifted, bed and all, into the sky. He was set down some distance away without his covers.

• A herd of sheep was "sheared" by a tornado. The animals were not hurt, just cold.

• A rooster was sucked into an empty 2-gallon jug unharmed.

Tornadoes have lifted whole buses filled with passengers, and then thrown them down to the ground. It's very common for houses to shatter or even rise into the air before being destroyed. The only safe thing to do is run for cover—in a deep basement, not in a vehicle or mobile home.

Miniature Hurricanes

Once you know about hurricanes, it's easy to understand a tornado. Like a hurricane, a tornado is a storm with circling winds and a "chimney" in the middle where the pressure is very low. (For that reason, tornadoes, like hurricanes, are often called "cyclones.") Like a hurricane, a tornado usually spins counterclockwise (above the equator), but some tornadoes spin in the opposite direction.

Unlike a hurricane, a tornado forms over land. Its powerful swirling winds destroy objects and then send the broken pieces of wood, glass, metal, and concrete speeding through the air. While a hurricane may measure hundreds of miles across with an eye that is 15 or 20 miles wide, a tornado is a much more compact storm. A mile across is large for a tornado; usually it's much smaller. The eye of a tornado is at the most 250 feet across.

Tornadoes have appeared on every continent.

Unlike hurricanes, they often arrive in groups. In April 1974, 148 tornadoes struck 12 different states, killing 315 people. In 1989, a total of 840 tornadoes struck the United States. Forty-eight people were killed.

A tornado has extremely low pressure in its eye. If a tornado passes right over a house that has all its windows and doors closed—and if the house has withstood the fierce winds—the eye's very low pressure may cause the building to explode. The pressure outside the house suddenly will be much lower than the pressure inside. The air in the house will expand instantly into the low pressure around the house. And the walls and roof will blow out as if someone had set off dynamite inside.

Funnel Cloud in the Distance!

It's simple—and terrifying—to recognize a tornado. It's a whirling black column of wind with its "head" above the clouds. It gets its color from the dust and broken objects that it churns up along its deadly path.

Often it has the shape of a funnel, wider at the top and narrow near the ground. But it might be straight up and down like a hose, or it might bulge in some places and pinch in others. Its whirling winds give it the nickname "twister."

A tornado doesn't always have the usual appearance. Some tornadoes are too close to the ground to be seen from a distance. And some tornadoes don't touch the ground at all, but they can do plenty of damage. The whirling winds scour a path along the ground while the funnel itself is hidden in the clouds above.

Tornadoes build up tremendous electrical charges. Frequently colorful lightning bolts can be seen around it. Inside the eye, lightning strikes constantly. The sound of booming thunder fills the air with a roar, like several locomotives racing together.

Selective Destruction

Within a single tornado there may be several smaller spinning columns. It might move through a neighborhood and wipe out a line of houses, but leave the houses across the street from the destruction untouched. A funnel might move 5 miles in one direction, then make a U-turn, and head back the way it came.

The town of Udall, Kansas, was hit by a "selective" tornado in May 1955. A policeman named Lester Thompson was driving home around ten o'clock at night when he was overtaken by a very heavy rainstorm. After passing through Udall, he came to a side road leading off the highway. He pulled onto the road so that he could find a place to wait out the storm. Finally he arrived at a farmhouse that had a few outbuildings.

Thompson sat in his parked car, in the pouring rain, facing the house. Suddenly the car began to shake in the wind. Through the rain-lashed windshield he saw the porch of the farmhouse move up and down, like a boat on a wave. Then the porch rose up and burst into pieces.

Thompson ran through the pounding storm to the house. There he found a family, badly cut by shattered glass, but still alive.

Right in front of Thompson's car the tornado pulled the porch off the house, scooped up the animals and outbuildings, but left the farmhouse untouched. Then it passed on. When the twister hit the town of Udall itself, it destroyed most of the buildings.

A party was being held that night at the town's community center. Just as people were getting ready to leave, they felt their ears popping. They heard the distant roar that signaled an approaching tornado. So everyone gathered against one wall of the room. When it hit, the tornado lifted the roof and knocked out three walls, leaving only one wall standing—the one where 12 women and children had taken cover. They were all safe.

In March 1984 a tornado struck a school in Alabama and damaged most of the classrooms, but it "skipped over" the school gym where more than 350 students were having a dance! The storm caused plenty of damage, but no injuries.

Tornado Watch

Scientists cannot do anything to prevent a future "monster" tornado from striking, but warning systems have improved. Experts keep track of vast amounts of information so that they can predict when conditions might lead to tornadoes. Volunteer "sky watchers" stay in touch with the weather forecasters. An unmistakable sign of a coming tornado is a sky full of greenish-black bubble-shaped clouds. Communications systems have improved to the point that people can be warned of approaching storms that are only minutes away.

An important tool for scientists who study tornadoes is a special kind of radar. *Doppler radar* lets scientists measure the speed and distance of particles within a thunderstorm. It also shows when water droplets and the wind that carries them are spinning. Often, Doppler radar can predict a tornado about 20 minutes sooner than the funnel actually appears, so there is more time to prepare for disaster.

But like volcanoes, earthquakes, and hurricanes, tornadoes are beyond human control. The mighty swirling winds, pounding rains, towering waves, explosive eruptions, and quaking plates are all an incredible display of nature's power. They help to shape and change the planet we call home.

AMERICAN QUASAR

AMERICAN QUASAR

poems

David Campos

Art by Maceo Montoya

 Red Hen Press | *Pasadena, CA*

Book design by Mark E. Cull

Library of Congress Cataloging-in-Publication Data

Names: Campos, David, 1984– author. | Montoya, Maceo, illustrator.
Title: American quasar : poems / David Campos ; art by Maceo Montoya.
Description: First edition. | Pasadena, CA : Red Hen Press, [2021]
Identifiers: LCCN 2021008411 (print) | LCCN 2021008412 (ebook) | ISBN
   9781597094481 (trade paperback) | ISBN 9781597098724 (epub)
Subjects: LCGFT: Poetry.
Classification: LCC PS3603.A49 A82 2021 (print) | LCC PS3603.A49 (ebook)
   | DDC 811/.6—dc23
LC record available at https://lccn.loc.gov/2021008411
LC ebook record available at https://lccn.loc.gov/2021008412

Publication of this book has been made possible in part through the financial support of Jim Wilson.

The National Endowment for the Arts, the Los Angeles County Arts Commission, the Ahmanson Foundation, the Dwight Stuart Youth Fund, the Max Factor Family Foundation, the Pasadena Tournament of Roses Foundation, the Pasadena Arts & Culture Commission and the City of Pasadena Cultural Affairs Division, the City of Los Angeles Department of Cultural Affairs, the Audrey & Sydney Irmas Charitable Foundation, the Kinder Morgan Foundation, the Meta & George Rosenberg Foundation, the Albert and Elaine Borchard Foundation, the Adams Family Foundation, the Riordan Foundation, Amazon Literary Partnership, the Sam Francis Foundation, and the Mara W. Breech Foundation partially support Red Hen Press.

First Edition
Published by Red Hen Press
www.redhen.org

Acknowledgments

Some of the following poems, including some of the images, have been published by the following magazines, some in different forms. Thank you, editors of the following publications, for sharing the work:

The Acentos Review, Atticus Review, Ploughshares, Prairie Schooner, and *Queen Mob's Teahouse.*

Contents

I
American House Fire

American House Fire   13

Even Under Pressure, There is No Indictment   16

The Human Condition is a Drought   17

Change   19

American Boy   20

My Tongue Has Been Sanded Down   22

Headstones   23

Your Country   24

Deep Into Election Night   26

Letter to Earth After "The Earthquake"   27

A Town Hall in America in Five Movements:

    I. Gun Silence   28

    II. The Condition of My Heart   29

    III. Restricted Love   30

    IV. The American Dream   32

    V. The Censorship of Teeth   33

Surveillance   34

America Responds in Headlines   35

This American House   37

Forever Renting   38

American Appropriation   39

American House Fire II   41

Even Knowing Its History   42

American Boy II   43

Historian of Buried Stars   45

The Archaeology of the Scales   47

II
Quasars

How an American Boy Becomes an Astronomer   53

The Vocabulary of the Sky   55

The Catastrophe of Men   57

Seeking the Perfect Stargazing Location, the Perfect Trail   59

Amateur Astronaut Thinks He Discovers the Meaning of Faith   61

Directions from an Archeologist   62

In the House of Libra   63

The Dormant Quasar in Our Center   64

The Discovery of a Quasar   66

Supernova   68

Letter to a Young Astronomer   70

After Years of Not, He Begins to Dream Again   73

In the House of Scorpio   74

Telescope at the End of the Universe   76

Name Games   77

Letter to My Brother   78

Slow Religion   79

Years Later   81

Physics at the End of the Universe   82

Something Like the Color of Faith   83

Notes   87

AMERICAN QUASAR

I

AMERICAN HOUSE FIRE

AMERICAN HOUSE FIRE

In a house fire, you don't die
from the flames, so don't mind the broken
windows. I'm trying to let the smoke out.

I have been for a long time running
from room to room looking for an exit.
What I would give for the chill of starlight,
to believe in a just god who brings rain

to temper the blaze ravaging my house,
to feel, for once, what it's like to win;
in victory, instinct orders our arms to rise

toward the heavens. Some say
this is what we're left with to remind us of god,
to remind us to surrender.
But the smoke has stolen

too many of our fathers; it's after our sons.
And every door leads to another dead dream's room.
Still, they watch my house burn,

smoke lifting its arms over the city.
Only if they didn't cook with fire, they say.
Only if their house had followed code.
How many more doors will have to burn

until it's yours? I'm running out of windows,
and my arms are losing their strength.
The sky darkens with victory,

surrender? It's hard to tell
anymore. But what's certain is
in a house fire, you die
when you cry your child's name.

Even Under Pressure, There is No Indictment

There are still patches of grass left
        clinging as if the soil was about to leave

for a place it rains, though clouds have teased
        of possibility. The grass is always greener

on the inside of myself where grass and bones are one—
        the sternum, the ribs, the blades, the iron,

the gate around the lawn; even inside my body the grass
        browns. No matter how much I've tried to protect

the small patches—they are still patches covering
        the holes in my chest bleeding soil everywhere.

The Human Condition is a Drought

A drought wreaks before I plant the body. I soften the soil with sorrow and sign the cross from muscle memory. I start with the spot on my forehead my mother kisses, end with the most sinful part of the body, the lips.

Have you ever rubbed the tough soil around the edges of your mouth? Had history just beyond the reach of your tongue? The *Book of the Dead* is the ground beneath our feet.

And it rains during this drought; though too many layers of soil have hardened. Each grain impossible to read. It will take years of above average rain to replenish the names.

Mathematics proves the sun will first expand and devour the inner planets before imploding; a star begins to collapse when iron manifests in its core; is this why people shoot each other?

Is this why the rain has stopped? Are there no more names left in our mouths? The only water left is in our blood; everyone hides a knife in their pocket.

Change

The boy on a bicycle begs for a hooked knife—
　　to buy a hamburger means the hunting season was good.

　　　　　A trail of blood leads to your front door while his mother collects
　　　　　razor blades and sends him out again.

A furnace of hands built your house
　　where every sheet of drywall remembers

　　　　　when it was cut from a distance. You try
　　　　　your steak knife; to finesse the truth

means you can afford thought.
　　You think, *The hesitant way love approaches*

　　　　　your hand. The sun's heat severs the "K" in knife—
　　　　　your comfort means a silent killing.

You can't recall the sound of sliced meat.
　　You tell yourself they bought hamburgers;

　　　　　a dull edge means it's of tired of killing.
　　　　　You hand out all your change.

American Boy

I dream myself young, running
    to adore the sky's color—
I'm white. Instead of myself,

        I wonder where all the blues went.
      They're not in the broken record player;
          the needle only plays songs of crushed bone.

I want to call out the sky's real name
    even though my tongue has been sanded down
from years of hushing my own.

        And I can't shake the tongueless boy
      knowing I will never grasp
        how to love myself in color.

everything kept inside

My Tongue Has Been Sanded Down

Now, I speak in the glances
        my father has given me
        in church; the communion goes
        uneaten. There is no tongue
        to taste salvation

when America has become better
        at dispensing misery.
        I hear it's like an alcoholic's memory
        of their first beer snuck
        while their father wasn't looking into himself.

Though it's no longer as bloody
        like when Columbus landed.
        It's as discreet as all the hooded men
        in our history books who disappeared

behind their managers' desk.
        From there, they take our mouths.
        How long has it been
        since they touched without taking?
        Don't confuse this slouch for a bow.

My skull has become heavier without lips.
        Everything kept inside writhes and piles.
        The desire for their names to be listed
        in the grains beneath our feet
        rises even higher than a tongueless Icarus.

Headstones

The lemon tree becomes its own headstone.
Still, the leaves rustle, unwilling to give up
their place. Perhaps, they wish spring,
a rain, a gentle sun to bring them back.

This is my fault for not saving gray water
because I could not give the plant secondhand anything
or even insult it with its history of chemicals.

The water was restricted, though neighbors cheated,
and I too could have to stop the transformation.

From my office window I watched the leaves
harden to granite as they watched me decay
into my complacent comfort. Though, perhaps,
we've always been stones.

Your Country

Call its name to bend time
until it bursts open like an orange
bitten without its rind.

There, where it bleeds like gouged sockets
where eyes used to be, the fresh odor of desire
without a leash paints straight stripes

with conquered ink. Does a tree remember
the bodies hung in its name?
Does the land remember

the languages it buried?
America, I'll snap you like cinnamon sticks,
throw you into a pot of boiling water,

and pour you into a porcelain cup.
This can't cure these feverish lips,
this body's ache. Your darkness

is too much like the centers of galaxies
surrounded by the protest of the stars
as they march into you in rebellion. Each night

forgiveness and ignorance mix
like blood and honey. Each night
two tablespoons before bed.

Deep Into Election Night

I toss to the out-of-tune rattle inside
       and rush to hush the darkness of the front porch.

It's just another trick whiteness used
       to swerve me into hushing myself.

Hush, little road, don't say you don't
       lead anywhere. All roads

end. Back to sleep I go, sent to
       reach under the bushes wondering

if the needle I saw there remembers
       everything it's been stuck into.

Letter to Earth After "The Earthquake"

Dear Earth: you shook my father's birth city. On the TV a camera no one had paid attention to that recorded the mundane of work caught people starting to run, caught the fear spreading across a man's face much like my own as if I too had forgotten how the earth moves, has moved. That underneath, my wounds too heal and split slowly.

Somehow, I'm supposed to find cover and cower under a desk because the magnitudes are exponential. In my sleep, will I even notice the love trying to wake me up? Sometimes I think I've forgotten how love continues to crush me.

Your layers crash into each other. Where things begin and end burden clarity. Even the reused needle picked up unknown vibrations. The San Andreas fault carves through drought and snow. Its fingers crave the fracture. Once, a train rolled by miles long tonguing the wound where the stitches held. But every year each inch breaks your face. All the houses crumble to collections of bone.

But I who did nothing to save even myself in the chaos remember all the fragments of this house. I blame the earthquake, the foundation, but never my own hands. David.

A Town Hall in America in Five Movements:

I. Gun Silence

When denied the essential: a sunrise—
Fog breaking to open sky—

       Hands will wait in their gloves
       For knives   for the cutting
       For the vines to fall
       All day gathering
       Food for other people's stomachs

So they too can enjoy the poisoned stillness
Of moments of silence, of thoughts and prayers.

II. The Condition of My Heart

When I used to go outside, I didn't look at the sun or admire its crown. But I bowed to its heat. The high-pressure system moved into my heart, melting sand.

Glass is just another form of rock, and my ribcage is as fragile as time. The kindness in a hug can crush me.

I wonder if my mouth has become crystal, if Chihuly blew my veins, bones, and fierceness and infected that place, those pockets inside my chest, if I'll be able to move and sharpen my tongue for war that will happen, that has happened, that I write into a journal and then burn the pages.

My neighbors have seen the smoke, had their eyes open and looking over the fence hoping to see the secret we're all chasing. *Do you know what sorrow is? And how it got here?*

All the mirrors are broken. And the sun refuses to show you my shadow.

III. Restricted Love

Inside the pockets of my chest
I carry an opportunity to lose myself
In another's caress. I remember, every finger
has a pair of eyes.
      I watch myself
smile the "devil's desire." *This is what laws say,
the Bible says.* Though my lover retorts, touch
is God's invention.

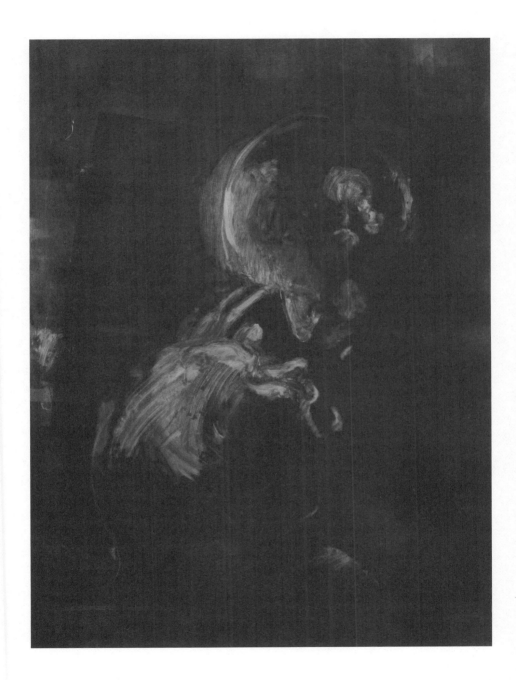

IV. The American Dream

When I dream of living well, my house is a home where all furniture has a name—where one could name its makers, and a kitchen where the talking is real and not full of pleasantries one says to keep from unfolding into bricks one wants to throw through blood's window.

All I want is my mother's room full of books in Spanish, my father's room—one he builds himself—above the garage, close to his hammer. Close my hammer, now and pray the nails haven't rooted.

V. The Censorship of Teeth

On a five-hour plane ride, the clouds opened
Their fists, slapped me until I was gums
And jaw bone—
      there, a failed root canal ate
      with an unquenchable hunger.
One can still scream without the mandible.

Surveillance

I bite my nails to stop from talking,
from pronouncing the disassembly
I witness everyday at work;
my students' eyes have not seen justice
since it left them at birth
without even a token to remember,
without walking from room to room
and placing its hand on the doorways
while everyone slept and dreamt of a place
where the hungry wouldn't have to bite
their nails for food. There is memory in
the accumulation of guilt like sediment
in a riverbed collecting bones and shit.

Rot is just another form of life
and who's to say there isn't any
underneath my eyes
underneath the violence of speaking,
of saying I love you and waiting
to hear it back, to echo, to understand.
I can try to save them if I only spoke up—
A terrible anxiety lives inside a paycheck.
Money is just another word for *Hush*.

America Responds in Headlines

It's not enough.
I'm still hungry.

All those headlines
were yesterday's profit.

Can't you see I'm willing to steal
your secret skins to wear,

make them pretty, make you believe
in your own dreams?

This American House

When I dream of America, it's only as big as a house, a home where all our roles are left on the doormat. I don't just wipe my feet, I scrape off the crumbs of my desires and leave as is my unkempt mouth.

There is no judgment. The angels do not descend and plague. Here, my mother's hands can still grasp the mug of coffee in her hands. My father's spine bends with ease and my brothers know what love is. And when they storm at me, they don't punch through the wall.

Though here, peace pushes a fist my into my chest. Here, my heart is a flock of mourning doves. And when I dream, I keep shooting them down from the powerlines.

Forever Renting

Does the wind have a home?
A place where it can wash itself,
build a fire, cook a meal of feathers
and leaves?

What I would give for a roof,
a ceiling with a fan, walls
with light switches, holes for cockroaches,
spider webs with daddy long legs,
a black widow curling its web
to lay its eggs, a little dog that barks
at the children outside playing tag

children with names like Juan
Juanita, Juan Carlos, Juan Gabrielle—
the roof and ceiling and everything that skitters
and scatters dances, sits, walks, kneels, and
begs.

This agony I rent from you
and only taste the small doses of relief
in the soft, soft pillow of mercy.

American Appropriation

We began with blood.
My metal takes more than flesh.
I've taken your name.

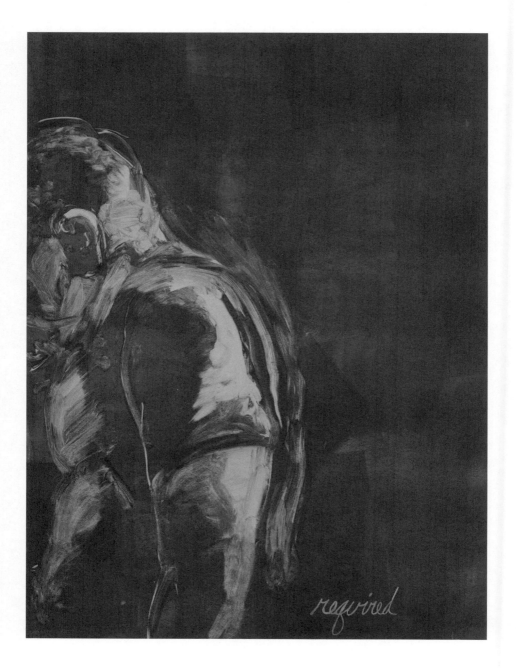

American House Fire II

After a house fire, there is no escaping
the ashes, the sneer of my charcoaled
fingers as I search for what's left.

I have been for a long time scouring
from pile to pile looking for a home.
What I would give for the calm of a roof
to shield from the searchlights of the stars

to compose that accusing gaze
to feel, for once, what it's like to be welcomed;
custom requires me to open my doors

to the wanting. Some say
this is what we're left with to remind us of god,
to remind us to surrender.
But the ashes have stolen

too many of our hands; it's after our voices.
And every flickering ember is a muffled scream.
Still, they watch my hands burn,

fingers digging for something clean.
Only if they didn't cook with fire, they say.
Only if their house had followed code.
How many more hands will have to char?

I'm running out of ashes. And soon
I'll be a field with no wind.

Even Knowing Its History

Even still, I dream the sun cresting,
its light removing the shadows,

the frost to reveal what's left
of the blossoms, to mourn what's died

what will die. I've stopped thinking
about you; this is about me.

Why am I so afraid of the sunrise?
The apocalypse doesn't have to be violent;

The horsemen are mirrors.

American Boy II

I've stopped dreaming.
Thankfully, and I have opened my eyes—
I am color. I am sure
everything is a box of crayons;
the blues lives here
inside this body of drums.
The needle is my tongue;
I remember my name

And want to call it out
that beautiful color,
the one that hid
between vineyard and whiskey
for years. I'm overwhelmed
with vowels, their hues;
I lick my fingers, my lips.
The sky adores me.

Historian of Buried Stars

I've spent too much time trying to decipher
the constellations. Their stories have lost

       their meaning in my mouth. The bull always rises
       my missing tongue from the dead,

then gores me until I remember their names—
names mean home mean a life spent searching

the sky digging through the earth
       for something that doesn't exist,

an illusion I've conjured
to deal with all our suffering.

How long has it been since you looked
       into a mirror and saw your true reflection?

Yesterday is already a setting constellation.
There must be something to why we compare eyes to stars.

       When we're gone, we'll just be a collection of memories.
       And then, later still, an emotion draping itself,

if only for a moment, over their eyes.
Admit you'll never understand yourself,

       how ugly you are, how beautiful.
       It was so much easier to believe

that everyone I buried became stars,
constellations we could point to and say

look! look at all those stories still living.

The Archaeology of the Scales

It's all about which tool   you choose to dig—

    The spade,   the pick,   your hands

have already done this   before you think

    in a previous life

        on a plain like this

           where the earth was hard

and as unforgiving   as your founding fathers.

When you dig   you can feel the belt

    of their stones   pummel you

    into the pieces of   the shame you've inherited.

Sometimes violence   is necessary

    for it to vanish.   First, it must pass

    through your body.

And so you heal   your fathers

    with your disobedience

and your acceptance

of their dying embers

in your palms.

This is how you discover   how perfect

your hands are   for digging   beyond them

and yourself

to find all the buried stars

inside the earth.

When you're almost nothing   but spirit and love,

you'll set them free   like fireflies

twinkling

their sighs of relief.

II
QUASARS

How an American Boy Becomes an Astronomer

He listens to his father groan

then laugh, then cry, then, silently, leave him

    without the blues   to carry him

to crack him   open   and spill his insides

all over a dancefloor.   He casts a resurrection spell

without language;   the whole body is a mouth.

He convinces himself   he's done the math

like Mrs. Hall taught in third grade; remember

to carry the remainders.   He's charted it out

on graph paper   like in Mr. Borjas's algebra class.

Though numbers cannot figure out all the dark matter

in his father's eyes,   his heart,

the center   of his galaxy, and what happens after death

what happens when someone disappears

    into star matter.

in the knife sky

The Vocabulary of the Sky

Patience smells first of fury

and then molten iron

cooled in arctic waters.

It looks like your father's face

as he passes, slower

than the blossoming between father and son.

Agony comes full of swagger,

wears too much cologne.

When you feel it swing through your hair

you remember the lice, his disapproval,

waiting to eat until you sleep.

You swear to be his opposite.

Ambition is perfect for flying kites

that won't twirl and tangle

in your father's stares; its direction clear

and as fulfilling as a glass of water

on the other side of the country.

The Catastrophe of Men

I learned to pray in an old cathedral
where angels wielded swords of fire.

The last time holy water dried on my forehead
my grandfather poured lizard blood

into the chalice of my body. Can you see

how broken my will is? Or is my will my undone body?
My undone faith? Did I quench the flames

when I swallowed the sword? Am I a house?
Am I my own house? Who will scream my name

trying to find me? Am I a cathedral?
If you enter me, can I relearn to pray?

Hombres somos lo que toman la sangre,
he said. But blood has many forms.

Hombres matan para comer, he said.
Murder is the language of our hands.

Seeking the Perfect Stargazing Location, the Perfect Trail

At night, I lay and cover myself with the ghost of nostalgia.
It's warmer than blankets.

At night, cold is just another visitor I tend to
just like my mother taught me—offer it something to drink,

offer it something to eat. At night, I do. As I stare
at the arms of light, I give it my warmth and fogging breath,

my dried and cracked lips, the shirt on my back,
the savings I hide in the bundle of my clothes

until I'm naked and shivering under its feet.
Still, at night, the cold wants more. Unsatisfied,

it takes a lump of hair and then one dream—
cold has no shame. Sensing weakness it just takes.

And I give. Each night, I give
until the stars find shelter in the horizon

and the trails grow coarse with grass and loose stones.

I continue to walk unsure of every step, wondering
if I'd ever find a place to set my telescope

wondering if the place I'm going to has been taught the same thing
about tending to company. At night, I give it my hope,

the one thing I hold on to the ways stars cling to their crowns
and wishes made upon them. And I, who am just a body

whose breath is all the wind and silence,
who gives all my dreams and clothes and words and fire,

arrive. I ask for nothing.
And I, who am just a body, a thing like many things

we learn to love and unlove with ease
finally finds a place, here, right here, in this burning.

Amateur Astronaut Thinks He Discovers the Meaning of Faith

Earth is riddled with craters;
      lakes are bandages and headstones
      without names.

When I shave, the scar on my chin
      sketches out how it was sewn
      back together and thrown into the sun

into a forty-five-mile drive to work
      coffee in hand and the grind of dairies
      filling the air and my mouth with manure

into hanging drywall all day
      building walls for other people's homes
      so they too can enjoy a hole

being punched in during Thanksgiving.
      When my brother says, *just because you're smart*
      doesn't mean you have to use it—

A scar is a body's offering, how it prays,
      even though I claim I don't.
      The Earth was made for knees.

Directions from an Archeologist

Pull your fingernails off.
Find out why you have been
trying to bite them off for so long.

They're useless anyways—
some leftover trait
in the leap of evolution.

Claws were once needed
to dig into the bark of trees
and climb to safety, to sleep

among the leaves, closer to the stars.
Some clawed through hide for meat.

They were as useful as teeth;
after childhood, you only get one set.
But your fingernails grow forever,

even after your death.
Even after your teeth have rotted,
they'll never be clean.

They'll never be your father
nor do they hide him
or the way he's leaving you now.

In the House of Libra

I.   The Poet Writes—

      A bird will always fly
      into your window
      and break its neck
      because sometimes
      guillotines are as clear as sky.

II.   The Student Writes—

      The bird is the speaker.
      The window is his father.
      The guillotine is his father leaving.
      The breaking of the neck
      is a metaphor for his emotional response.

III. The Poet Responds to the Student—

      I used to live in an apartment
      with a floor-to-ceiling window
      with my desk pushed against the glass.
      Every now and then I would hear the thud
      of a body slam and fall
      onto the woodchips for the cats.

IV.   The Father Responds to the Student and the Poet—

      My love has always been the bird.

The Dormant Quasar in Our Center

I snap photos of the sky, label them in permanent marker—
Orion, Taurus, Pluto, Sagittarius A.

Everything ends up on a star map,
even the dirt. I collect slowly and try to remember

if what I saw in the nights before were true.
So I throw myself onto the telescope,

press my face against the finder,
and breathe. Tell me where love goes

when it's gone. Please. Tell me
the unraveling sky hides no stars.

Tell me it gives all its breath to the empty.

The Discovery of a Quasar

I can't even fathom the stars' numbers.
If only I was just another soul curious and blind,

I would not understand how the light waves lie,
bend the truth when a star chokes on iron.

An astronomer ain't much different from a coroner.
Hope styles our hands as we're caught looking straight

into a body. I have a tale to tell. Want to hear
when my heart stopped?

It started like myths—the rings came in pulses,
like a lover's voice whispering the apple into your hands.

Supernova

After Yusef Komunyakaa

As a kid, I searched for father's matchbooks,
anywhere he would smoke:
his work truck, the backyard—
the bench he built from scrap wood,
and the kitchen where Mom shooed
him away, though the smoke lingered.
The smoke always lingers and stains.

I found and lit them one by one
stared into them before I tested
the distance between palm and
burning. In Mexico, I held
bean sparklers between my fingers.
They spewed into the street as I ran.

Last week, the smoke from the Rough Fire
stampeded into my city and stayed too long.
It rained ash and weakened the sun
long enough to stare into its red heart;
My father still believes I will become the star
to rest his last wishes on; all of them collapse
under their own weight. I've been preparing

for the departure, for the Enola Gay
to rise into the sky directly over my chest—
the little boy inside loves fireworks too.
Perhaps this is why we gather on Independence Day,
why we'll sit silently in our folding chairs
waiting for dusk to disappear
for the long coat of stars to drape themselves
over the land, for the thunder of something leaving

．

the earth to shake us. *And watch the darkened sky light to make us whole again.*

Letter to a Young Astronomer

Beyond your city and love, out there
in the unfathomable cold
the brightest stars burn with frostbite.

Zoom in and find rapture,
exile in a dilapidated solar system
where the planetary bodies that didn't fit

their expectations float and twirl
in their own menace.

But here, here you'll grow ill
if you don't uncover your eyes
because this is still part of your city,
the love that has always been yours
to unsee through the hands
you've carried and worn,
tattered and now full of holes.

There is no kindness in not witnessing
the approach of your own death—

Still, you're here with chilled skin,
looking beyond the empty branches
of the tangerine tree to the warm glow
a street lamp gives you.

You've been cutting lungs in the dark
and now and only just now do you walk
underneath the lamp's umbrella

to embrace sight. Dig with those irises.

The archeology has only just begun.
Already, you've found ancient tools—
sharpened bones and stones

dug out for drinking the blood
from the sky heart. Everything you find in mirrors
becomes as bright and as beautiful as the city
and love where your tangerines grow,

a hardened bark armoring the trunk
and branches full of green to drink the sun

until the stars of orange bulb out from their misery
in drought—bitter, sweet, or anything in between.
Savor, but forget the expected,
the required ingredients for licking your lips,
and accept all the planets
toxic and furious, solid or gas,
unbearable and welcoming
like your first slice of tangerine.

And wonder why, oh why
you had hidden for so long.

After Years of Not, He Begins to Dream Again

My tongue dries out, my teeth crumble.
      Sand belongs on beaches, in playgrounds, but I wonder

if my mouth has become both, if Dali visited my beginning,
      my now, and my future and infected those places

if I'll be able to scream or make those quiet sounds of lovemaking
      that will happen, that has happened, that I've tried to keep

to myself when the walls were thin and I knew my neighbors
      had their ears pressed against the walls, hoping to hear the secret

we'll all chasing. Do you know what love is? And how to get there?
      Lately, all I've known is the waking hours . . .

The frost settles on my car and lawn, the sun warms—
      But, oh, at night, at night the cold of the stars.

In the House of Scorpio

Cut me, Scorpion.
The stubble has grown too long—

    a goat is what you kill
    and bury in the dirt to cook.

Scorpion, my razor is dull.
I have new blades
but I don't use them.

I want to see the blood
when I cut
feel the warmth run free

from the body,
    fall back to the dirt

to the dirt to the dirt
to the dirt to the dirt.
I grab a handful of hair
from the sink and

    consider eating it.
When I washed the goat's face
    I knew I wanted to kill for so long.

    Grandfather, do you remember
    asking me to hold the goat still
    for the knife. Mijo, you said, no te dejes.

This is how I learned to eat.

the angels did not descend

Telescope at the End of the Universe

The mirrors reached the conclusion of light;
night had swallowed everything and reigned
like the king of entitlement. This is how

they say the universe will die. Faith
presents a second opinion—one with angels
descending from the sky with horns and fire.
Perhaps our death is somewhere in between
erudition and the cross.

I confided in machinery, became imagination's ruin,
trusted in priest, so my curiosity was led to a coffin.
In the viewfinder, my reflection but a small pixel.

Name Games

After Mark Statman

Pops, you hate your name, Ildeberto,
so you left behind the excess weight.
You're Beto. Two syllables. Beh-toh, now
you can't lift too much anymore
which means, soon, I will carry you
into your name and, later, into mine.

And I know my name,
inherited, means fuck you.
And this unibrow, too, inherited
which I pluck and shave
means fuck you too,
which also means
I inherited your chipped tooth,
your weak teeth,
and the holes in your mouth,
so when I smile, fuck you.

So fuck you means David
These syllables you punched your father with
when he abandoned you with your uncle David;
so David really means father
which really means papi
which really means love me.

How many more games
will we play with our names
until it's over? Even Campos means
fields with stunted trees.

Letter to My Brother

You burnt a cigarette into my arm
because your heart had broken and you wanted
to fight her dad in the driveway. You gave

me silence again. Thank you
for the small scar, its oval shape.
I wish I could paint the way you do,
the geyser flowing knuckles without abandon
out from your shoulder with purpose,
that deep sigh Dali stole from you.

                    When you sent
those bones for me and hit wall instead,
I wonder if you rejected painting your masterpiece.

The hole you punched into the wall
was a perfect oval as if you'd studied
sculpting with your fist. Months of silence
followed again. I appreciate the time
I had to watch paint dry over the patch.

Slow Religion

This is what your father's arms say when they hold you:
What if yesterday broke open like your face did
in your parents' dining room, and no one looked—
no one important—at your slow rapture? What if
yesterday dragged its fingers across this city
and into the next plucking those high electric wires,
music falling out of each socket,
but all you heard was the slow religion
of your mouth, the syncopated breaths
between sobs? And what if yesterday embraced
the terror of resentment like your lips did?
What if yesterday was nothing but a husk, the leftovers
you keep wrapping in tin foil and keeping inside
the fridge? What if you acknowledged yesterday,
the cold, and the way things slow down
right before impact? What if today's wreckage
began to study music again: Middle C, the major
chords, sweaty palms on a first date, a kiss
on the lips, no longer just pecks of memory?
What if through the wreckage you learned
the architecture of music? What if the wreckage,
the carnage, the catastrophe, was your music?

Years Later

I've telescoped the light of myself—
The body speaks in star language;
Its music on the verge of supernova.

But I'm learning to touch from the stars—
Those who've suffered the Big Bang;
Each night, a lesson on how life happens.

Now, each touch of the body, a reach
Into potential grief, each curve
A signal from the undiscovered dark.

Physics at the End of the Universe

You walk through bookstores with your new love
And every book's title is an ending
In another language.

In another language
An ending walks with your new books
As if every love was a failing title

Because every love is a flailing title.
Books can walk all over language
With the same tongue,

Kiss with the same tongue.
Language loves to linger before a lie.
Before you grab a spine

And after you hold a spine
Lie about the linger's purpose.
To discover the truth,

To uncover your truth,
Walk through a bookstore in love
With the spine of your new language.

Something Like the Color of Faith

Each sunrise is a church.
Yesterday morning, alcohol dripped
from my breath, a bead of sweat
from a woman's brow teetered on my shoulder—
the warmth of her lips leaving my neck. The sun
so bright I confused this for love.

I bought her flowers, an arrangement—
the intelligent colors of spring,
had them delivered to her work
left a note to remind her
of the way she held my throat
and squeezed, how it made me laugh,
not in the way three people walk into a bar,
but in the way death appears when a life is taken
says, "I need a place to stay."

        But this madrugada,
I drive into the farmlands again
to teach the making of a sentence
where I think I'm certain
what constitutes a complete thought.
Perhaps I believe it the way my students do
when I draw it out on the whiteboard.
Blue marker. Red marker. Purple noun. Green verb.
The bright sun over the valley, yellow.
No, gold. No, something like the color of faith.

I roll down my windows, smell the manure,
and believe in the education of the wind rushing past me;
a sky diver right before the jump—

right before I say "I love you" again;
remember how loud it is to
give all of yourself. When I say it,
I understand what it means to pray.

Notes:

"Supernova" borrows its ending sentiment/idea from Yusef Komunyakaa's "Ode to the Drum."

"Name Games" borrows a move from Mark Statman's "My Name."

Biographical Notes

David Campos is the son of Mexican immigrants, a CantoMundo fellow, and the author of *Furious Dusk* (University of Notre Dame Press, 2015), which won the Andrés Montoya Poetry Prize. His poems and other work have appeared in *Prairie Schooner,* the *American Poetry Review, Ploughshares,* and *Queen Mob's Teahouse,* among many others. He teaches English at Fresno City College. For more information, visit his website at www.davidcampos.me.

Maceo Montoya's paintings, drawings, and prints have been featured in exhibitions and publications throughout the country as well as internationally. He has published three works of fiction, *The Scoundrel and the Optimist* (2010), *The Deportation of Wopper Barraza* (2014), and *You Must Fight Them: A Novella and Stories* (2015), as well as *Letters to the Poet from His Brother* (2014), a hybrid book combining images, prose poems, and essays. His most recent publication is *Chicano Movement for Beginners,* a work of graphic nonfiction. Montoya is an associate professor in the Chicana/o Studies Department at UC Davis. More information about his work can be found at www.maceomontoya.com.